SPANISH EYES
MOON LIGHT AND ROSES
108 As Time Goes BY

SPANISH EYES
MOON LIGHT AND ROSES

108 As Time Goes BY

A READER'S DIGEST SONGBOOK

THE EASY WAY TO PLAY
100 UNFORGETTABLE HITS

Editor: William L. Simon
Music arranged and edited by Dan Fox
Senior Staff Editor: Mary Kelleher
Designer: Judy Speicher
Staff Editor: Eileen Hughes
Music Associate: Elizabeth Mead
Illustrations by John Martinez
Rights Manager: Lisa Garrett Smith

♪

READER'S DIGEST GENERAL BOOKS
Editor in Chief: John A. Pope, Jr.
Managing Editor: Jane Polley
Executive Editor: Susan J. Wernert
Art Director: David Trooper
Group Editors: Will Bradbury, Norman B. Mack, Kaari Ward
Group Art Editors: Evelyn Bauer, Joel Musler
Chief of Research: Monica Borrowman
Copy Chief: Edward W. Atkinson
Picture Editor: Richard Pasqual
Rights and Permissions: Pat Colomban
Head Librarian: Jo Manring

THE READER'S DIGEST ASSOCIATION, INC.
Pleasantville, New York/Montreal

Reader's Digest Fund for the Blind is publisher of the Large-Type Edition of *Reader's Digest.* For subscription information about this magazine, please contact Reader's Digest Fund for the Blind, Inc., Dept. 250, Pleasantville, N.Y. 10570.

Index to Sections

Index to Songs

How This Book Helps You to Play Real Music

We believe that anyone — well, *almost* anyone — can play music. And we believe that with this new-style songbook from Reader's Digest, more people than ever before will be able to sit down and plunk out some of the best popular songs ever written.

The Easy Way to Play 100 Unforgettable Hits has been designed primarily for two groups of people: those who have very limited piano skills and those who are enjoying that newest fun machine, the electronic keyboard. If you play another instrument, you can use the book too, as you'll see when you read on. Whatever the instrument, everything is designed to let you play the melodies you know and love with the very least effort and with the utmost comfort and convenience.

To start with, there are the 100 melodies themselves. Every song in this book is, indeed, an unforgettable hit. All have been performed and recorded by many different stylists, both vocal and instrumental, and by different types of orchestras, from swing to sweet to symphonic. You'll find the glorious melodies and lyrics of such

composers as George and Ira Gershwin, Richard Rodgers and Oscar Hammerstein, Cole Porter, Walter Donaldson, Jerome Kern, Alan Jay Lerner and Frederick Loewe, and Irving Berlin.

You will find just a few contemporary songs here. The reason for this is that many songs from the 1970s and '80s don't translate comfortably to a solo piano or keyboard: Their complex rhythms and bass guitar lines can't be duplicated without considerable effort, and the electronic effects that can be produced on a recording cannot be approximated. All of the songs here stand on their own as *melodies*.

The songs that we have included are songs that have endured, and will continue to endure, for generations. And all have been made easy — and fun — to play by Dan Fox, the master arranger of every Reader's Digest music book. All sound full and rich.

Now read on a bit, take a quick look at the few sample bars of "As Time Goes By" printed below and discover just how this book can work for you.

Keyboard players! Anything printed in blue is especially for you
Black print is for easy piano and more experienced players

For Electronic Keyboards

Anything printed in blue is designed especially for you. This includes the top line of the music — the treble, or right-hand, clef — with the notes numbered for those who can't read music, as well as the suggested tempos, rhythms and colors (more about these later). Of course, if you can play the piano and use your electronic keyboard with both hands, just as you do an acoustic piano keyboard, it's advisable to play the full-scored piano arrangements for bass and treble clefs, printed in black. See the section on "Easy Piano" that follows for further information.

For chords to accompany the melody, look to the letters, also printed in blue, above the keyboard line. (The simplest, inexpensive monophonic [one-note-at-a-time] models of keyboard will not play chords.) For this and other instructions, *please consult the manual that came with your instrument.* The notes that can sound automatic chords will probably be identified on the backboard behind the keys of your instrument. But to help you find them, you can use the peel-off stickers with letter names that are provided with this book. (See "About the Stickers" on the following page.) You don't have to know what notes constitute each chord; just press the indicated key with your left hand. For a simple major chord you usually press one key or button. For example, to play a C chord, press a C in the designated bass portion of the keyboard, below Middle C. That

key will automatically play the three notes of a C chord (C, E and G). If you want a D chord (D-F#-A), just press a D. To play minor chords or major and minor 7th chords (indicated in the music by such notations as Cm, G(7), Gm(7), and so on), you may have to use two, three or four fingers of your left hand. Different makes of keyboards require different techniques. For example, on a Casio, to play a minor chord, such as Cm, you play the C plus any neighboring note directly above the C. On a Yamaha, you would play the C plus any note *below* the C. If your instrument does not play 7th chords, you can still get a satisfactory harmony with the basic chord — say, a G rather than a G(7). In fact, the parentheses around the 7 indicate that the 7th chord is optional. *Again, consult your manual.*

At the top right-hand corner of the first page of each song, we have suggested tempos, rhythms and instrumental colors for that tune. Always remember that our suggestions are just that — *suggestions.* As you become more familiar with the keyboard, you'll begin to experiment with the music, and you'll have fun choosing your own instrumental sounds and different rhythms for a song.

Counting time. If you know how the song goes, you will probably know how long each note should be held — even if you don't know a half-note from a quarter-note. We don't go into musical notation here. However, we do show you where the beats are by the red marks underneath the lyrics; each mark (▾) is to be counted as one beat. Your electronic keyboard probably has a tempo light that blinks on each beat, so you can coordinate with that — one ▾ for each blink.

Automatic rhythms. The rhythms you can use on a song depend on the make and model of your instrument. Some electronic keyboards can play a polka rhythm; others cannot. Some have a "cha-cha" button, others a "bossa nova." Some can combine two rhythms to sound like a rhythm they don't have on a single button. Again, study your manufacturer's manual. And experiment.

Instrumental colors. Most keyboards offer piano, flute, guitar, strings, organ and a few other instrumental sounds, or colors. Some of the more versatile models allow you to mix different colors, which may enable you to come closer to the actual instrument sounds, or even to create your own sounds. Once again, consult your manual, since different makes offer different choices.

Once you know your keyboard and its many possibilities, you may be able to simulate an orchestral arrangement even if you are not a trained musician. Certainly your satisfaction will come easier and faster than you ever dared to dream, and you'll have great fun getting there. And remember, players on electronic instruments have a great advantage: you can play with earphones, and no one has to hear what you're doing until you're ready to turn on the amplifier and dazzle them.

Easy Piano

Perhaps you're a piano student, or a retiree who is "getting back" to the piano after not touching it for most of your adult years. Or you're a wind instrument player who always wanted to "play a little piano." Then our very easy two-hand arrangements, printed in black, are for you. (The melody line, printed in blue, is for electronic keyboards.)

Since some players may have little experience with the bass, or left-hand, clef, our arrangements never ask you to play more than a single note at a time with your left hand. The name of each bass

note is printed in red under the lines, under each note. Until you grow more familiar with the bass notes, you can use the peel-off stickers to identify the notes in the two octaves from Middle C down. You might also find the beat marks (▾), printed in red, helpful.

More experienced players can refer to the chords that we've indicated at the top of the piano lines, in black. These chords are sometimes different from those on the keyboard, or blue, lines, substituting more complex harmonies that are not in the automatic chord bank of electronic keyboards.

For Non-Keyboard Players

If you play a single-note instrument, such as a violin, flute, saxophone, clarinet, oboe, trumpet, harmonica or melodica, you can play from the electronic keyboard melody line (printed in blue), reading the notes. However, if you want to play in combination with another instrument, you would have to be sure that the other instrument is pitched in the same key. Clarinet, trumpet and tenor or soprano saxophone, for example, are B-flat instruments and can play together from the same music. Piano, guitar, accordion, autoharp, violin, flute, oboe and some recorders are in C. Alto and baritone saxophone and mellophone are in E flat, and so on.

If you play accordion or autoharp, you can certainly play from the blue lines; but depending on the options your particular instrument provides, you might get more variety out of the harmonies in the piano staves, printed in black. *Guitarists* can begin with the simpler chords of the blue lines and then graduate to the chords in black.

It's conceivable to us that different members of your household may use these arrangements in different ways at different levels of proficiency — the more the merrier.

Now, let's play the music! And perhaps you'd like to start with our musical illustration, the timeless "As Time Goes By." Go ahead, try it. See if Dooley Wilson, who played it in *Casablanca,* has anything on you. It's on page 108.

—*The Editors*

Middle C

About the Stickers

A set of peel-off stickers for the keys of your piano or electronic keyboard is included with this book. The diagram above shows how to position them.

The numbered stickers are primarily for electronic keyboard players who can't read music. If you are in this category, you will be playing the top line of the music, printed in blue. These are the treble, or right-hand, notes.

The lettered stickers are for two octaves of notes in the bass, or left-hand, clef — to the left of Middle C — on both electronic keyboards and pianos.

To position the labels of the right-hand notes on your instrument, first find Middle C, which will be Number 1. It is in the center, or just to the left of center, of the keyboard, the first white key below the grouping of two black keys.

Then the black key directly up from C, or C sharp (C♯) (which is the same as D flat [D♭]), becomes 1+. D becomes 2. D sharp (D♯), the same as E flat (E♭), becomes 2+, and so on, following the diagram.

Notes in the bass clef are identified by their letter names rather than by numbers. Position them as shown on the diagram. Starting on the C two octaves below Middle C, the white keys will read C-D-E-F-G-A-B and repeat again up to 1 (Middle C). The black keys will read C♯/D♭, D♯/E♭, F♯/G♭, G♯/A♭, A♯/B♭, until you reach the F♯/G♭, G♯/A♭ and A♯/B♭ just to the left of Middle C. The stickers will identify these as F+, G+ and A+. The reason for this is that the melody sometimes reaches down to those keys below Middle C, and, for non-music-readers, this is consistent with the 1+, 2+ identifications of the melody from Middle C upward.

DREAM

Words and Music by Johnny Mercer

Slow and steady   TEMPO: Moderate   RHYTHM: Rhumba, Bossa Nova   COLOR: Strings, Flute

Dream_____ when you're feel-in' blue._____

Dream,_____ that's the thing to do._____ Just_____

_____ watch the smoke rings rise in the air;_____ You'll find your share_

Dream a Little Dream of Me

Words by Gus Kahn; Music by Wilbur Schwandt and Fabian Andre

8

I Left My Heart in San Francisco

Words by Douglass Cross; Music by George Cory

TEMPO: Moderate   RHYTHM: Bossa Nova   COLOR: Electric Piano

IN THE MOOD

Music by Joseph Garland

Lindy (♪♪ played as ♪³♪)   TEMPO: Moderate   RHYTHM: Swing, Big Band   COLOR: Reed ensemble, Sax or Brass ensemble

13

LOVE LETTERS IN THE SAND

Words by Nick and Charles Kenny; Music by J. Fred Coots

TEMPO: Slow   RHYTHM: Rock   COLOR: Rock Guitar

Slowly

On a day like to - day, we passed the time a -

way writ - ing love let - ters in the sand. How you

laughed when I cried each time I saw the tide take our

love let - ters in the sand. You made a

14

Words by Johnny Burke; Music by Erroll Garner

TEMPO: Slow   RHYTHM: Slow Rock, Bossa Nova   COLOR: Jazz Organ, Strings way, and a thou-sand vi – o – lins be – gin to play, or it might be the

sound of your hel – lo, that mu – sic I hear. I get mist – y the mo – ment you're

near. You can say that you're lead – ing me on,

but it's just what I want you to do. Don't you no – tice how

Misty

Star Dust

Chorus - in tempo, slowly

Some-times I won-der why I spend the lone-ly night dream-ing of a song; The

mel - o - dy haunts my re-ve-rie, and I am once a-gain with you, when our

love was new and each kiss an in-spir-a - tion. But

that was long a-go; Now my con-so-la-tion is in the star dust of a song. Be -

SATIN DOLL

Words by Johnny Mercer;
Music by Duke Ellington and Billy Strayhorn

Moderate swing

TEMPO: Moderately fast   RHYTHM: Swing, Big Band   COLOR: Jazz Organ, Piano no - bod-y's fool so I'm play - ing it cool as can be;_____ I'll

give it a whirl,_but I ain't for no girl_catch-ing me. Switch-e-roo-ney

Tel - e-phone num - bers, well, you know. Do-ing my rhum - bas

with u-no and that 'n' my sat - in doll.

23

Seems Like Old Times

Words and Music by Carmen Lombardo and John Jacob Loeb

TEMPO: Moderate   RHYTHM: Swing, Big Band   COLOR: Sax, Clarinet, Flute

Seems like old times, hav-ing you to walk with. Seems like old times, hav-ing you to talk with. And it's still a thrill just to have my arms a-round you; Still the thrill that it was the day I

IT'S ALL IN THE GAME

Words by Carl Sigman; Music by Charles Gates Dawes

Moderately slow

TEMPO: Moderately slow   RHYTHM: Waltz   COLOR: Celeste, Vibraphone

Too Young

Words by Sylvia Dee; Music by Sid Lippman

TEMPO: Moderate   RHYTHM: Big Band, Rhumba   COLOR: Vibraphone, Accordion

Fly Me to the Moon

Words and Music by Bart Howard

TEMPO: Moderately slow   RHYTHM: Waltz   COLOR: Strings, Flute

Fill my heart with song and let me sing for - ev - er - more;

You are all I long for, all I wor - ship and a - dore. In

oth - er words,_____ please be true;_____ In

oth - er words,_____ I love you.

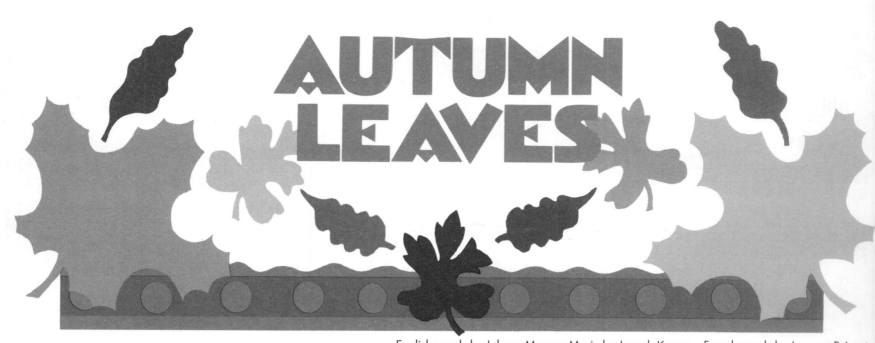

AUTUMN LEAVES

English words by Johnny Mercer; Music by Joseph Kosma   French words by Jacques Prévert

TEMPO: Moderate   RHYTHM: Rhumba, Bossa Nova   COLOR: Strings, Flute

IT'S A SIN TO TELL A LIE

Words and Music by Billy Mayhew

TEMPO: Moderate   RHYTHM: Swing, Big Band   COLOR: Saxophone, Accordion

I'm Gonna Sit Right Down and Write Myself a Letter

Words by Joe Young; Music by Fred E. Ahlert

ALL OF ME

Words and Music by Seymour Simons and Gerald Marks

TEMPO: Moderate to Fast   RHYTHM: Swing, Big Band   COLOR: Brass ensemble

Red Sails in the Sunset

Words by Jimmy Kennedy; Music by Hugh Williams

TEMPO: Moderate   RHYTHM: Rhumba, Slow Rock   COLOR: Strings, Flute, Harmonica

40

The Very Thought of You

Words and Music by Ray Noble

Moderately slow, with a lilt

TEMPO: Moderately slow   RHYTHM: Big Band, Swing   COLOR: Clarinet, Flute

Lyrics:
The ver-y thought of you and I for-get to do the lit-tle or-di-na-ry things that ev-'ry-one ought to do. I'm liv-ing in a kind of day-dream; I'm hap-py as a king. And fool-ish though it may seem, to me that's ev-'ry-thing. The mere i-

I Found a Million Dollar Baby
(in a Five and Ten Cent Store)

Words by Billy Rose and Mort Dixon; Music by Harry Warren

TEMPO: Moderate   RHYTHM: Big Band, Swing   COLOR: Sax, Trombone

These Foolish Things
(Remind Me of You)

Words by Holt Marvell; Music by Jack Strachey and Harry Link

TEMPO: Very slow   RHYTHM: Big Band, Swing   COLOR: Strings, Organ

46

you. You came; You saw; You con-quer'd me.

When you did that to me, I knew some-how it had to be.

The winds of March that made my heart a danc-er; A tel-e-phone that rings, but who's to an-swer.

Oh, how the ghost of you clings; These fool-ish things re-mind me of you.

TENDERLY

Words by Jack Lawrence; Music by Walter Gross

TEMPO: Very slow   RHYTHM: Waltz   COLOR: Strings

Slow waltz

The eve-ning breeze ca-ressed the trees ten-der - ly. _____ The trem-bling

trees em-braced the breeze ten-der - ly. _____ Then

you and I came wan - der - ing by, and

lost in a sigh were we. _____ The shore was

kissed by sea and mist ten-der-ly. I can't for-

get how two hearts met breath-less-ly. Your

arms o-pened wide and closed me in-side. You took my

lips; You took my love so ten-der-ly.

49

FOOLS RUSH IN

Words by Johnny Mercer; Music by Rube Bloom

TEMPO: Moderate   RHYTHM: Rhumba (Beguine)   COLOR: Flute, Strings

Slow and steady

Fools rush in where an-gels fear to tread; And so I come to you, my love, my heart a-bove my head. Though I see the dan-ger there; If there's a chance for me, then I don't care.

WHAT'S NEW?

Words by Johnny Burke; Music by Bob Haggart

TEMPO: Moderately slow   RHYTHM: Beguine, Big Band   COLOR: Trumpet, Strings

You Go to My Head

Words by Haven Gillespie; Music by J. Fred Coots

TEMPO: Slow   RHYTHM: Rhumba, Bossa Nova   COLOR: Flute, Clarinet, Horn

Ballad

You go to my head, and you lin-ger like a haunt-ing re-frain;

And I find you spin-ning round in my brain like the bub-bles in a

glass of cham-pagne. You go to my head like a sip of spark-ling bur - gun - dy brew; And I find the ver-y men-tion of you like the kick-er in a

ju - lep or two._____ The thrill of the thought that you might give a thought to my

plea casts a spell o - ver me. Still I say to my-self, "Get a hold of your-self. Can't you

see that it nev - er can be?" You go to my head with a smile that makes my

58
ALL THE THINGS YOU ARE
Jerome Kern and Oscar Hammerstein wrote this gorgeous tune in 1939 for *Very Warm for May*. The show flopped, but "All the Things You Are" became a standard—because it's all the things a great song should be.

60
EMBRACEABLE YOU
George and Ira Gershwin's 1930 musical *Girl Crazy* overflowed with great songs—"I Got Rhythm," "But Not for Me," "Bidin' My Time" and this lovely ballad, with George's charming melody and Ira's intricate lyrics.

62
TEA FOR TWO
Vincent Youmans and Irving Caesar's cheerful little earful became an instant success in 1924 when it was introduced in *No, No, Nanette*. It's been performed in many styles, including a hit cha-cha version in 1958.

64
NIGHT AND DAY
He didn't have much of a voice—but few other movie stars have introduced as many wonderful songs as Fred Astaire. Cole Porter wrote the luscious "Night and Day" for Fred to sing in *The Gay Divorce* (1932).

67
I'VE GOT A CRUSH ON YOU
Only a genius like Ira Gershwin could put together words like "crush," "mush," "coo" and "woo" and come up with a popular standard. He performed the feat for his and brother George's 1928 musical *Treasure Girl*.

68
APRIL IN PARIS
Even if you've never been there, "April in Paris" seems to bring back memories of the City of Light. Vernon Duke and E.Y. Harburg (he had never been to Paris either) wrote the song in 1932 for *Walk a Little Faster*.

70
HELLO, DOLLY!
What do Carol Channing, Ginger Rogers, Martha Raye, Betty Grable, Pearl Bailey, Phyllis Diller, Ethel Merman, Barbra Streisand and Louis Armstrong have in common? Why, "Hello, Dolly!" of course. The ladies all portrayed Dolly Gallagher Levi, and Satchmo had a hit recording of this title tune.

72
YOU DO SOMETHING TO ME
Cole Porter's *Fifty Million Frenchmen* opened on Broadway a month after the stock market crash in 1929. Despite the general gloom, songs such as "You Do Something to Me" made the show Porter's first big hit.

74
'S WONDERFUL
'S wonderful, 's marvelous. 'S by George and Ira Gershwin. This sibilant, slurring song, sung by Adele Astaire, sister of costar Fred, was one of the features of the Gershwin brothers' 1927 musical *Funny Face*.

76
THE MAN I LOVE
"The Man I Love" is a show tune that became popular without being heard on Broadway. It was dropped from two Gershwin shows (*Lady Be Good* and *Strike Up the Band*), but ear appeal turned it into a standard anyway.

78
DANCING IN THE DARK
"People seem to enjoy dancing in the dark," Guy Lombardo told Arthur Schwartz and Howard Dietz, as he lowered the lights at the Roosevelt Grill. A few nights later, the songwriters returned and asked Guy to play... guess what? The song appeared in their 1931 revue *The Band Wagon*.

80
DANCING ON THE CEILING
Richard Rodgers and Lorenz Hart's "Dancing on the Ceiling" was first heard in their London musical *Ever Green* (1930). The set for the show-stopping number featured a huge, upturned chandelier rising from the stage floor.

82
SEPTEMBER SONG
This autumnal song is from Kurt Weill and Maxwell Anderson's *Knickerbocker Holiday* (1938). It was sung—half-sung, you might say—by Walter Huston, who played aging Peter Stuyvesant, in love with a young girl.

84
SMOKE GETS IN YOUR EYES
There's less and less cigarette smoke around these days to get in your eyes, but let's hope there will always be smoke from smoldering passions and hearts on fire. Jerome Kern and Otto Harbach's lovely song first saw the light of day in *Roberta*, in 1933.

86
WITH A SONG IN MY HEART
Rodgers and Hart left us with many songs in our hearts—none more heartwarming than this one, from their 1929 Broadway show *Spring Is Here*. Singer Jane Froman made the song her own in the early 1940s.

88
MY HEART STOOD STILL
Richard Rodgers and Lorenz Hart were riding in a taxi in Paris when they almost collided with another car. "My heart stood still," a companion exclaimed. The duo featured their new song in *A Connecticut Yankee* (1927).

90
LOVE ME OR LEAVE ME
Torch singer Ruth Etting introduced this ultimatum in 1928 in *Whoopee*, a lavish Florenz Ziegfeld show that starred Eddie Cantor and featured another Walter Donaldson–Gus Kahn classic, "Makin' Whoopee."

92
LOVER, COME BACK TO ME
Sigmund Romberg and Oscar Hammerstein's *The New Moon* (1928), the story of a French aristocrat in colonial America, was one of the last swashbuckling operettas written for Broadway. The lush score included this yearning ballad.

94
STOUTHEARTED MEN
Few could beat Nelson Eddy for stoutheartedness. And fewer yet could resist him when he sang this rallying call in the 1940 film version of *The New Moon*. Other standards from the show: "Lover, Come Back to Me," "Wanting You" and "Softly, As in a Morning Sunrise."

96
SOMEONE TO WATCH OVER ME
George Gershwin conceived this ballad as a jazzy dance number but soon realized his mistake. A forlorn Gertrude Lawrence, clutching a rag doll in her arms, sang the plaintive plea in the Gershwins' *Oh, Kay!* (1926).

98
SEND IN THE CLOWNS
In recent years, fewer and fewer songs from Broadway shows have gone on to become standards. One that did was Stephen Sondheim's poignant "Send In the Clowns," from his 1973 musical *A Little Night Music*.

102
TOMORROW
Leapin' lizards, Sandy! Nowadays Little Orphan Annie is better known on Broadway than she is in newspaper comic strips. The curly-topped redhead first sang this anthem to the near future in *Annie* in 1977.

ALL THE THINGS YOU ARE

From *Very Warm for May*   Words by Oscar Hammerstein II; Music by Jerome Kern

TEMPO: Moderate to Fast   RHYTHM: Big Band, Bossa Nova   COLOR: Jazz Organ, Sax, Clarinet

Embraceable You

From *Girl Crazy*   Words by Ira Gershwin; Music by George Gershwin

TEMPO: Slow   RHYTHM: Swing, Bossa Nova   COLOR: Strings, Sax

60

Tea for Two

From *No, No, Nanette* Words by Irving Caesar; Music by Vincent Youmans

TEMPO: Moderately slow RHYTHM: Pops, Cha Cha COLOR: Muted Trumpet

With a lilt

Pic - ture you up - on my knee, just tea for two and

two for tea; Just me for you and you for me a - lone.

No - bod - y near us to see us or hear us, no friends or re - la-tions on

week-end va - ca - tions; We won't have it known, dear, that we own a tel - e -

NIGHT AND DAY

From *The Gay Divorce*   Words and Music by Cole Porter

TEMPO: Moderate   RHYTHM: Rhumba, Beguine   COLOR: Strings, Flute

Night and day_____ you are the one,_____ on-ly you be-neath the moon and un-der the sun._____ Wheth-er near to me or far, it's no mat-ter, dar-ling, where you are, I think of you_____ night and day._____

I'VE GOT A CRUSH ON YOU

From *Treasure Girl* and *Strike Up the Band* Words by Ira Gershwin; Music by George Gershwin

67

April in Paris

From *Walk a Little Faster*   Words by E. Y. Harburg; Music by Vernon Duke

TEMPO: Slow to Moderate   RHYTHM: Swing   COLOR: Clarinet, Sax

HELLO, DOLLY!

From *Hello, Dolly!*   Words and Music by Jerry Herman

TEMPO: Fast RHYTHM: Swing, Big Band COLOR: Trumpet, Reed Synth.

YOU DO SOMETHING TO ME

From *Fifty Million Frenchmen* Words and Music by Cole Porter

TEMPO: Fast RHYTHM: Swing COLOR: Piano, Jazz Organ

'S Wonderful

From *Funny Face*   Words by Ira Gershwin; Music by George Gershwin

TEMPO: Moderately fast   RHYTHM: Swing, Big Band   COLOR: Jazz Organ, Trumpet

Lyrics:
'S won - der - ful,_____ 's mar - vel - ous,_____ you should care _____ for me._____

'S aw - ful nice,_____ 's par - a - dise,_____ 's what I love _____ to see. _____ You've

The Man I Love

From *Strike Up the Band* Words by Ira Gershwin; Music by George Gershwin

TEMPO: Very slow RHYTHM: Swing or Pops, or no rhythm COLOR: Flute, Oboe, Accordion

Slowly

C · Cm · Gm · Bbm

5 6 5 6 5 6+ 5 6 5 6+ 5 6 5 6 5 6+ 4 5 4 6

Some-day he'll come a-long, the man I love; And he'll be big and strong, the man I love;

C · Cm · Gm · A+
C · C · Bb · A

Fm · G(7) · C · G(7)

4 5 4 5 4 5+ 3 4 3 5 4 3 3 3

And when he comes my way, I'll do my best to make him stay.

Fm · G7 · Cmaj7 · C#dim · D9 · G7
Ab · G · C · G · F# · F

C · Cm · Gm · Bbm

5 6 5 6 5 6+ 5 6 5 6+ 5 6 5 6 5 6+ 4 5 4 6

He'll look at me and smile, I'll un-der-stand; And in a lit-tle while he'll take my hand;

C · Cm · Gm · A+
C · C · Bb · A

Fm · G(7) · C · Fm · C · E

4 5 4 5 4 5+ 3 4 3 5 3 1 1 1

And though it seems ab-surd, I know we both won't say a word.

Fm · G7 · C · Fm · C · E7
Ab · G · F · E · F · E · D

76

Copyright © 1924 (Renewed) WB Music Corp.

Dancing in the Dark

From *The Band Wagon*   Words by Howard Dietz; Music by Arthur Schwartz

TEMPO: Moderate   RHYTHM: Swing, Big Band   COLOR: Jazz Organ, Sax, Jazz Guitar

Look - ing for the light _____ of a new love to

bright - en up the night, _____ I have you, love, and

we can face the mu - sic to - geth - er.

Danc - ing in the dark. Danc - ing in the dark.

much slower

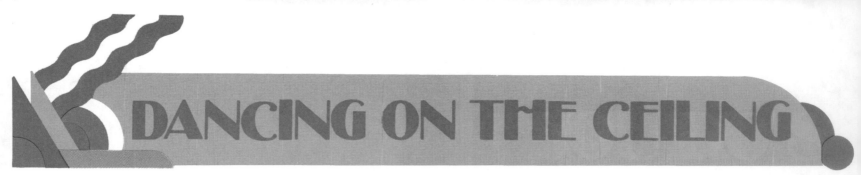

DANCING ON THE CEILING

From *Ever Green*   Words by Lorenz Hart; Music by Richard Rodgers

TEMPO: Moderately slow   RHYTHM: Cha Cha, Pops   COLOR: Muted trumpet, Flute

I whis - per, "Go a-way, my lov - er, it's not fair."

But I'm so grate-ful to dis-cov - er he's still there.

I love my ceil - ing more since it is a danc - ing floor

just for my love.

much slower

September Song

From Knickerbocker Holiday   Words by Maxwell Anderson; Music by Kurt Weill

Moderately slow

TEMPO: Moderately slow   RHYTHM: Bossa Nova or Beguine   COLOR: Cello

Oh, it's a long, long while from May to De - cem - ber,

but the days grow short when you reach Sep - tem - ber. When the au-tumn

weath - er turns the leaves to flame, one has-n't got

time for the wait - ing game. Oh, the

days dwin-dle down _____ to a pre - cious few, _____ Sep-

tem - ber, _____ No - vem - ber! And these few

pre - cious days I'll spend with you; These pre - cious

days I'll spend with you. _____

83

Smoke Gets In Your Eyes

From *Roberta*   Words by Otto Harbach; Music by Jerome Kern

TEMPO: Slow   RHYTHM: None, play freely   COLOR: Strings

So I chaffed them and I gai-ly laughed to think they could doubt my love.

Yet to-day my love has flown a - way, I am with - out my love.

Now laugh-ing friends de - ride tears I can-not hide; So I smile and

say, "When a love-ly flame dies, smoke gets in your eyes."

small notes opt.

small notes – optional ending

85

With a Song in My Heart

From *Spring Is Here*   Words by Lorenz Hart; Music by Richard Rodgers

TEMPO: Moderate   RHYTHM: Rhumba, Big Band   COLOR: Flute, Strings

My Heart Stood Still

From *A Connecticut Yankee*   Words by Lorenz Hart; Music by Richard Rodgers

TEMPO: Moderate   RHYTHM: Rhumba, Beguine   COLOR: Strings, Flute

Love Me or Leave Me

From *Whoopee*   Words by Gus Kahn; Music by Walter Donaldson

TEMPO: Moderately fast   RHYTHM: Swing, Big Band   COLOR: Sax, Trombone

LOVER, COME BACK TO ME

From *The New Moon* Words by Oscar Hammerstein II; Music by Sigmund Romberg

TEMPO: Slow RHYTHM: 16 Beat COLOR: Strings

Slowly

The sky was blue and high a-bove; The moon was new, and so was love.

This ea-ger heart of mine was sing - ing, "Lov-er, where can you be?"

You came at last, love had its day; That day is past, you've gone a-way.

This ach-ing heart of mine is sing - ing, "Lov-er, come back to me." When

Stouthearted Men

From *The New Moon*   Words by Oscar Hammerstein II; Music by Sigmund Romberg

March tempo   TEMPO: Moderate   RHYTHM: March; or manually strike chord note on every beat   COLOR: Trumpet

Someone to Watch Over Me

From *Oh, Kay!*   Words by Ira Gershwin; Music by George Gershwin

TEMPO: Slow   RHYTHM: Rhumba or Pops   COLOR: Flute or Strings

SEND IN THE CLOWNS

From *A Little Night Music*   Words and Music by Stephen Sondheim

TEMPO: Moderate   RHYTHM: Rhumba   COLOR: Guitar

TOMORROW

From *Annie*   Words by Martin Charnin; Music by Charles Strouse

TEMPO: Medium fast   RHYTHM: Pops   COLOR: Clarinet

102

105
ALL THE WAY

"All the Way" went all the way to Best Film Song of 1957 and a million-selling recording for Frank Sinatra. Sammy Cahn and Jimmy Van Heusen wrote it for Sinatra to sing in *The Joker Is Wild*, the life story of Joe E. Lewis.

108
AS TIME GOES BY

Oh, come on. You *must* remember this. Morocco, 1941. Rick's Café Américain. Bergman and Bogart, and Dooley Wilson playing "As Time Goes By." Movies don't come any better than *Casablanca*, and songs don't come any better than this one.

110
BORN FREE

John Barry is best known for his brassy, rhythmic scores for such James Bond films as *Goldfinger* and *Thunderball*. He proved he could write softer stuff when he composed this sweeping Oscar-winning theme for *Born Free* (1966), a tremendous hit for pianist Roger Williams.

112
WHEN YOU WISH UPON A STAR

It's trivia time! Who sang this Academy Award-winning song in Walt Disney's *Pinocchio* in 1940? Give up? It was Jiminy Cricket, with a voice supplied by Cliff "Ukulele Ike" Edwards, a vaudeville star of the 1920s.

114
THREE COINS IN THE FOUNTAIN

Romance in Rome was the theme of *Three Coins in the Fountain*, and Sammy Cahn and Jule Styne came up with the perfect title song (an Oscar-winner) for the 1954 film. The "fountain" is the Fontana di Trevi. Legend has it that anyone who throws a coin into its waters is bound to return to the Eternal City. Try it and see.

116
DAYS OF WINE AND ROSES

It's a sad story, more about wine than roses. But the 1962 movie, starring Jack Lemmon and Lee Remick, will be remembered forever, thanks in part to Henry Mancini and Johnny Mercer's bittersweet Oscar-winning title theme.

118
I ONLY HAVE EYES FOR YOU

Harry Warren and Al Dubin wrote many film scores together—*42nd Street*, *Gold Diggers of 1933* and *Dames* among them—all containing many wonderful songs. Dick Powell sang "I Only Have Eyes for You" to Ruby Keeler in *Dames* (1934).

120
THE GLORY OF LOVE

Boston-born Billy Hill is known for his cowboy tunes—"The Last Roundup," "Wagon Wheels" and "Empty Saddles" among them—but his Eastern upbringing came through on "The Glory of Love." The song first became popular in 1936, hit again in 1967 after it it was used in *Guess Who's Coming to Dinner*, and yet again in 1989 when Bette Midler sang it in *Beaches*.

122
IT'S MAGIC

Doris Day made her reputation as a big-band singer with Les Brown and His Orchestra. Sammy Cahn and Jule Styne suggested her for a role in *Romance on the High Seas* (1948), in which she sang the composers' magical "It's Magic," and the rest is Hollywood history.

124
THEME FROM *A SUMMER PLACE*

Max Steiner's theme was the best thing about the soapy *A Summer Place* (1959). It became a best-selling recording for Percy Faith and His Orchestra—a recording that is to summer what Bing Crosby's "White Christmas" is to Christmas.

126
SEPTEMBER IN THE RAIN

Those leaves of brown have been tumbling down since 1937, when singer James Melton sang this lovely song in *Melody for Two*. It's another in the series of film tunes by the team of Harry Warren and Al Dubin.

128
THE WAY WE WERE

Just remember: We're not getting older, we're getting better. But it's always fun to look back on the way we were. Alan and Marilyn Bergman and Marvin Hamlisch's fond glance at the past, the title song of the Barbra Streisand–Robert Redford film, won an Oscar as Best Song of the Year in 1973.

131
THAT'S ALL

Among the records New York disc jockey–songwriter Bob Haymes played on his show was one of a melody he had written, called "C'est Tout." A fan call from Nat King Cole prompted Haymes to ask his friend Alan Brandt to supply lyrics for the tune. The result was this fine song, a fine recording for Cole and a fine addition to *Tootsie* 30 years later, in 1982.

ALL THE WAY

From *The Joker Is Wild* Words by Sammy Cahn; Music by Jimmy Van Heusen

Slowly, but with a lilt (♩♩ played as ⌐³⌐)

TEMPO: Slow RHYTHM: Bossa Nova, Pops COLOR: Piano, Strings

All the Way

AS TIME GOES BY

From *Casablanca*   Words and Music by Herman Hupfeld

TEMPO: Slow   RHYTHM: Big Band, Swing   COLOR: Sax, Piano

Moon-light and love songs nev-er out of date; Hearts full of pas - sion, jeal-ous-y and hate;

Wom - an needs man and man must have his mate, that no one can de - ny. It's

still the same old sto-ry, a fight for love and glo-ry, a case of do or die.

The world will al-ways wel - come lov - ers, as time goes by.

From *Born Free*   Words by Don Black; Music by John Barry

TEMPO: Moderate   RHYTHM: Rhumba or Beguine   COLOR: Flute, Strings, Guitar

Stay free,_____where no walls di – vide you,_____you're free as a

roar – ing tide so there's no need to___ hide._____

Born free,_____and life is worth liv – ing,_____but on – ly worth

liv – ing 'cause you're born free._____

When You Wish Upon a Star

From *Pinocchio*   Words by Ned Washington; Music by Leigh Harline

TEMPO: Slow   RHYTHM: 16 beat   COLOR: Strings

Three Coins in the Fountain

From *Three Coins in the Fountain*

Words by Sammy Cahn; Music by Jule Styne

TEMPO: Moderate   RHYTHM: Bossa Nova   COLOR: Oboe, Strings

Which one will the foun-tain bless? Which one will the foun-tain bless?

Three coins in the foun-tain, through the rip-ples how they shine.

Just one wish will be grant-ed; One heart will wear a val-en-tine. Make it

mine! Make it mine! Make it mine!

From *Days of Wine and Roses*   Words by Johnny Mercer; Music by Henry Mancini

TEMPO: Moderate   RHYTHM: Rhumba, Beguine   COLOR: Strings

I ONLY HAVE EYES FOR YOU

From *Dames*   Words by Al Dubin; Music by Harry Warren

TEMPO: Moderate   RHYTHM: Rhumba (Beguine)   COLOR: Strings

THE GLORY OF LOVE

From *Guess Who's Coming to Dinner*   Words and Music by William Hill

TEMPO: Moderate   RHYTHM: Swing, Big Band   COLOR: Trumpet, Sax, Jazz Organ

With a lilt

long as there's the two of us we've got the world and all its charms. And

when the world is through with us we've got each oth-er's arms. You've got to

win a lit-tle, lose a lit-tle, and al-ways have the blues a lit-tle:

That's the sto-ry of, that's the glo-ry of love.

IT'S MAGIC

From *Romance on the High Seas*

Words by Sammy Cahn; Music by Jule Styne

TEMPO: Slow   RHYTHM: Bossa Nova   COLOR: Flute, Piano

Slowly

C ... **Dm**

11 11 10 10 9 9 8   8 9 9 8 8 7 7 6   5   2

You sigh, the song be-gins, you speak and I hear vi-o-lins, it's mag - ic.

C ... **E♭dim** **Dm7** **G7**

f

C   G   E   E♭   D   F

G(7)

9 9 8 8 7 7 6   6 7 7 6 6 5 5 4

The stars de - sert the skies and rush to nes - tle in your eyes, it's

Dm7 (Echo) **G7**

p   *f*

D   F   G   D   G

C ... **Dm**

5   3   1 3 5 6 8 6   8 7 5   6

mag - ic. With-out a gold-en wand or mys-tic charms,

C ... **Dm7**

mf

C   G   C   C   G   C   E   D   C   B   G

D **G(7)**

2 4 6 9   10 9 8 7 6 7 8   9

fan-tas-tic things be-gin when I am in your arms.

Am7 **D7** **Dm7** **Fm6** **G7**

A   D   A   D   C   D   C   A   G   A♭   G   G

When we walk hand in hand the world be-comes a won-der-land, it's mag - ic.

How else can I ex-plain those rain-bows when there is no rain, it's

mag - ic. Why do I tell my-self these things that hap-pen are all real - ly

true? When in my heart I know the mag-ic is my love for you.

Words by Mack Discant; Music by Max Steiner

TEMPO: Slow   RHYTHM: Rock and Roll No. 1   COLOR: Strings

124

September in the Rain

From *Melody for Two*   Words by Al Dubin; Music by Harry Warren

TEMPO: Moderate   RHYTHM: Swing, Bossa Nova   COLOR: Brass Ensemble

THE WAY WE WERE

From *The Way We Were*   Words by Alan and Marilyn Bergman; Music by Marvin Hamlisch

Slowly

TEMPO: Slow   RHYTHM: Disco, 16 beat   COLOR: Piano, Organ

128

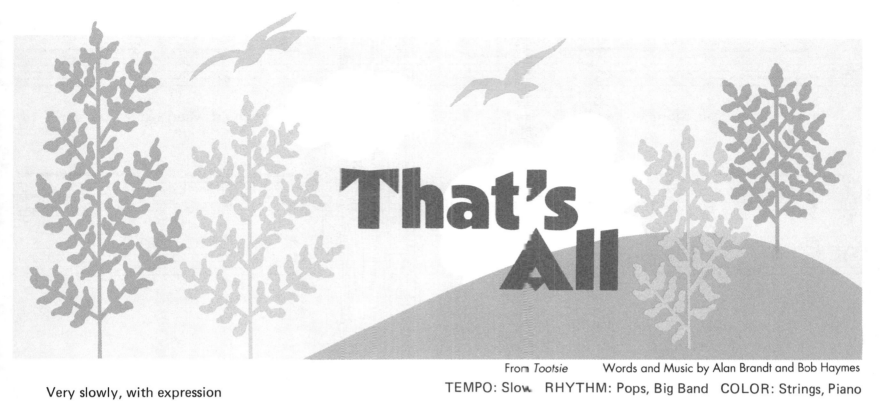

That's All

From *Tootsie* Words and Music by Alan Brandt and Bob Haymes

TEMPO: Slow RHYTHM: Pops, Big Band COLOR: Strings, Piano

Very slowly, with expression

That's All

135
I DON'T KNOW WHY (I JUST DO)

In 1931, the great songwriting team of Fred Ahlert and Roy Turk turned out "Where the Blue of the Night (Meets the Gold of the Day)," which Bing Crosby co-wrote and made his theme song, and "I Don't Know Why"— which sparkled even brighter and oftener because *everybody* sang it.

136
MEAN TO ME

Here's another hit by Ahlert and Turk. Written in 1929, it was one of the last great torch songs of the '20s. Not surprisingly, it was a hit for the two great torch singers of the period, Helen Morgan and Ruth Etting.

138
YOU MADE ME LOVE YOU

Songwriters Joe McCarthy and James Monaco made us love this song—ever since 1913, when Al Jolson introduced it on Broadway. Judy Garland sang it in *Broadway Melody of 1938*, and Harry James recorded it in 1941, with hints of both Jolson and Garland in his trumpet phrasing.

140
FOR ME AND MY GAL

Songwriters can be businessmen too, you know. When George W. Meyer was asked why he composed "For Me and My Gal" in 1917 (along with Edgar Leslie and E. Ray Goetz), he answered, "I was writing songs for a living and I needed the money." By the way, lyricist Leslie borrowed the title from the last line of another golden oldie, "Shine On, Harvest Moon."

142
DANNY BOY

Here's a song that has brought a tear to many an eye—and not just Irish ones. The melody became known as "Londonderry Air" after it appeared in print for the first time in 1855 in a collection put together by a Miss J. Ross of Londonderry. It wasn't until 1912 that Fred E. Weatherly gave the air the words that made it "Danny Boy."

144
SIDE BY SIDE

Duos—of singers, comedians, dancers—have been performing "Side by Side" ever since Harry Woods wrote it in 1927. Kay Starr followed the trend when she made her hit recording in 1953. Her partner? Herself: she overdubbed her own voice.

146
MY BLUE HEAVEN

Composer Walter Donaldson was a bachelor when he and George Whiting wrote this paean to married life in 1927. The tune was a tremendous hit for singer Gene Austin that same year. The modest Austin once said: "The most important element in the success of a record is the song, not the singer. I got an old sayin': 'Hit songs don't care who sings 'em.' "

148
MY BUDDY

Walter Donaldson again, this time with lyricist Gus Kahn. The two clicked with this touching waltz, their first collaboration, in 1922. Realizing that they had a good thing going, they went on to create such other standards as "Carolina in the Morning," "Yes Sir, That's My Baby," "Makin' Whoopee" and "Love Me or Leave Me."

150
BYE BYE BLACKBIRD

Ray Henderson and Mort Dixon's "Bye Bye Blackbird" came along in 1926. The song—a favorite of singing comedians Eddie Cantor and Georgie Price—was one of 10 hits that Henderson wrote in 1925 and 1926, among them "The Birth of the Blues," "Five Foot Two," "Alabamy Bound," "I'm Sitting on Top of the World" and "Black Bottom."

152
APRIL SHOWERS

Buddy De Sylva wrote the words for three of Al Jolson's greatest hits—"Avalon," "California Here I Come" and "April Showers." Jolson introduced "April Showers" (the melody was by Louis Silvers) in the Broadway musical *Bombo* in 1921 and continued to sing it throughout his career.

154
POOR BUTTERFLY

John Golden wrote the lyrics of "Poor Butterfly" in 1916, basing them on the plot of Puccini's opera *Madama Butterfly*. (Raymond Hubbell supplied the melody.) Stage star Sophye Bernard's performance of the song in *The Big Show*, an extravaganza at New York City's Hippodrome, turned the graceful ballad into one of the era's biggest hits.

156
I'M LOOKING OVER A FOUR-LEAF CLOVER

Mort Dixon teamed with Harry Woods to write this happy, jaunty 1920s song. It's been a favorite of the banjo-and-mandolin bands that march in Philadelphia's annual Mummers' Parade ever since, and was a good-luck charm for bandleader Art Mooney, who copied the string bands' style for a hit recording in 1947.

158
ALEXANDER'S RAGTIME BAND

Can you name five songs written by the great Irving Berlin that begin with the letter A? Hint: "Alexander's Ragtime Band" was the first one...way back in 1911. Others that you're sure to know are "All Alone," "All by Myself," "Anything You Can Do" and the immortal "Always."

160
ARE YOU LONESOME TONIGHT?

What is a country song like "Are You Lonesome Tonight?" doing in a group of old-time tunes, you ask? Well, sure, Elvis Presley had a huge hit with it in 1960, but in fact the song was written back in 1926 by Tin Pan Alley veterans Roy Turk and Lou Handman, who probably had no idea what "country music" was.

162
TILL WE MEET AGAIN

This charming waltz by Richard Whiting and Raymond Egan, published in 1918, was one of the hit songs of World War I. It was the first of a string of successes by composer Whiting (father of singer Margaret) that included "The Japanese Sandman," "Sleepy Time Gal" and "Beyond the Blue Horizon."

164
SHINE ON, HARVEST MOON

Let's hope that vaudevillians Nora Bayes and Jack Norworth had some inkling that they were writing perhaps the ultimate singing-round-the-campfire song when they created "Shine On, Harvest Moon" in 1908. Norworth also wrote the words of another perennial seasonal favorite: "Take Me Out to the Ball Game."

165
TOO-RA-LOO-RA-LOO-RAL (THAT'S AN IRISH LULLABY)

Before there was Bing Crosby (who sang "Too-Ra-Loo-Ra-Loo-Ral" to that leprechaun of a priest, Barry Fitzgerald, in *Going My Way* in 1944), there was Chauncey Olcott. Singer-songwriter Olcott specialized in sentimental Irish airs. He popularized James Royce Shannon's "Irish lullaby" (in 1914) as well as his own classics, "My Wild Irish Rose," "When Irish Eyes Are Smiling" and "Mother Machree."

I DON'T KNOW WHY

(I Just Do)

Words by Roy Turk; Music by Fred E. Ahlert

TEMPO Moderately Slow   RHYTHM: Swing, Big Band   COLOR: Jazz Organ, Trombone

MEAN TO ME

Words and Music by Roy Turk and Fred E. Ahlert

TEMPO: Moderate   RHYTHM: Swing, Big Band   COLOR: Trumpet, Sax

Light and swingy

YOU MADE ME LOVE YOU

Words by Joseph McCarthy; Music by James V. Monaco

For Me and My Gal

Words by Edgar Leslie and E. Ray Goetz; Music by George W. Meyer

TEMPO: Moderate   RHYTHM: Swing   COLOR: Strings

DANNY BOY

Words by Fred E. Weatherly; Music Traditional

TEMPO: Moderate   RHYTHM: Rhumba or Swing   COLOR: Flute, Strings

Moderately

142

SIDE BY SIDE

Words and Music by Harry Woods

Moderately (♪♪ played as ♪³♪) TEMPO: Moderate RHYTHM: Big Band, Swing COLOR: Banjo, Honkytonk Piano

Oh, we ain't got a bar-rel of mon - ey, may - be we're rag-ged and fun - ny, but we'll trav-el a - long sing-in' a song side by side.

Don't know what's com-in' to - mor - row, may - be it's trou-ble and sor - row, but we'll trav-el the road shar-in' our load side by side.

MY BLUE HEAVEN

Words by George Whiting; Music by Walter Donaldson

Nice and easy

TEMPO: Moderately fast   RHYTHM: Big Band   COLOR: Trumpet, Clarinet, Sax smil - ing face, a fire - place, a co - zy room, _____ a

lit - tle nest that's nes - tled where the ros - es bloom. _____ Just Mol - lie and

me _____ and ba - by makes three, _____ we're hap - py in

my blue heav - en. _____

147

My Buddy

Words by Gus Kahn; Music by Walter Donaldson

Waltz

TEMPO: Moderately slow RHYTHM: Waltz COLOR: Music Box, Violin, Vibraphone

* For a charming "music box" effect, play both hands an 8va higher.

148

Miss your voice, the touch of your hand, just

long to know that you un - der - stand, my

bud - dy, my bud - dy, your

bud - dy miss - es you.

Bye Bye Blackbird

Words by Mort Dixon; Music by Roy Henderson

Moderate singalong tempo   TEMPO: Moderate   RHYTHM: Big Band, Swing   COLOR: Trumpet, Clarinet, Trombone, Jazz Organ

April Showers

Words by B.G. DeSylva; Music by Louis Silvers

Smoothly

TEMPO: Moderate   RHYTHM: Big Band, Swing   COLOR: Strings, Clarinet

POOR BUTTERFLY

Words by John L. Golden; Music by Raymond Hubbell

Moderately slow

TEMPO: Moderately slow   RHYTHM: Swing, Rhumba   COLOR: Strings, Flute

155

I'm Looking Over a Four-Leaf Clover

Words by Mort Dixon; Music by Harry Woods

TEMPO: Fast   RHYTHM: Big Band, Swing   COLOR: Trumpet, Banjo

156

ALEXANDER'S RAGTIME BAND

Words and Music by Irving Berlin

Moderate swing (♫ played as ♪. ♪)

TEMPO: Moderately fast   RHYTHM: Swing, Big Band   COLOR: Sax, Jazz Organ

Are You Lonesome Tonight?

Words and Music by Roy Turk and Lou Handman

TEMPO: Moderate   RHYTHM: Waltz   COLOR: Organ, Strings

Moderately

Are you lone-some to-night? Do you miss me to-night? Are you sor-ry we drift-ed a-part? Does your mem-o-ry stray to a bright sum-mer day, when I kissed you and called you sweet-heart? Do the

TILL WE MEET AGAIN

Words by Raymond Egan; Music by Richard Whiting

TEMPO: Slow to moderate   RHYTHM: Waltz   COLOR: Strings, Harmonica or Accordion

Slow waltz

SHINE ON, HARVEST MOON

Words and Music by Nora Bayes and Jack Norworth

TEMPO: Moderate   RHYTHM: Big Band, Swing   COLOR: Banjo, Harmonica

Too-ra-loo-ra-loo-ral

(That's an Irish Lullaby)

Words and Music by James Royce Shannon

Moderately, with expression

TEMPO: Moderate RHYTHM: Disco COLOR: Panpipe, Flute

167
AMAZING GRACE

John Newton's poem, written as part of a sermon in 1779, has become one of the most popular hymns of all time. Newton, by that time an ordained minister in the Anglican church, had been captain of a slave ship for many years—and was rescued from that life by the power of grace.

168
HOW GREAT THOU ART

Although it dates back more than 100 years, "How Great Thou Art" is one of the most recent—and most popular—of religious songs. It was written in 1886 by a Swedish missionary, but was not translated into English until 1948, by the Reverend Stuart K. Hine. It became popular in the 1950s, thanks to George Beverly Shea, who sang it often during the Billy Graham Crusades.

170
WHISPERING HOPE

We're indebted to Philadelphian Septimus Winner for such odes as "Where Oh Where Has My Little Dog Gone," "Listen to the Mocking Bird," "What Is Home Without a Mother?" and—in a more tranquil vein—"Whispering Hope." He published "Whispering Hope" in 1868, under his mother's maiden name, Alice Hawthorne, presumably thinking the song's tender sentiments more feminine than masculine.

172
ROCK OF AGES

Augustus Toplady's beloved hymn "Rock of Ages," written in 1776, has consistently been among the top five favorite gospel songs. It was set to its present tune by the American composer and teacher Thomas Hastings in 1832.

173
PRAISE GOD FROM WHOM ALL BLESSINGS FLOW

Thomas Ken, an Anglican bishop, was royal chaplain to one British king, prisoner in the Tower of London of another. He will always be remembered for this simple four-line stanza, which he wrote in 1674 for a prayer manual. The sturdy tune it is set to, called "Old Hundredth," was composed by Louis Bourgeois and published in 1551.

174
IN THE GARDEN

In 1912, C. Austin Miles experienced a spiritual vision in which he saw Mary Magdalene and Jesus in the Garden of Gethsemane, where Jesus was buried. Miles awoke from his trance inspired to write the poem for this timeless gospel favorite. He added the music that night.

175
SHENANDOAH

Was "Shenandoah" named for a river in Virginia, a valley, an Indian maid or an Indian chief? The origins of the haunting song are clouded by time. Over the past two centuries, different versions of it have been sung by lumberjacks, river-barge men and sailors on the original tall ships. Our thanks to all of them.

176
GOODNIGHT, IRENE

Huddie Ledbetter, or Leadbelly, the legendary singer-guitarist from Louisiana, learned "Goodnight, Irene" from his uncle. He had been singing it for years when he first recorded it, for a Library of Congress folk-song project, in 1933. Leadbelly always believed the song could become a hit. He died in 1949, a year before The Weavers' recording became just that.

178
GREENSLEEVES

Legend has it that the oft-married English king Henry VIII wrote "Greensleeves." Whether he did or not, it's a regal tune. At Christmastime, the hymn "What Child Is This?" is sung to the melody.

180
I CAN'T STOP LOVING YOU

Many Nashville songwriters strive for years to come up with a hit song; Don Gibson managed to write two country classics in one afternoon: "I Can't Stop Loving You" and "Oh, Lonesome Me." The songs provided Gibson with a double-sided No.1 hit in 1958. "I Can't Stop Loving You" was also a big success for another country singer, Kitty Wells, and for rhythm-and-blues star Ray Charles.

182
TENNESSEE WALTZ

Pee Wee King and Redd Stewart's "Tennessee Waltz" was one of the first country and western songs to become a pop music hit, thanks to Patti Page's 1950 recording. Even though it's about a broken romance, not about the virtues of Tennessee, the ballad is now the official song of the Volunteer State.

184
DON'T FENCE ME IN

Guess who takes credit for this tune of the wide-open spaces? None other than Yale man Cole Porter, one of the most sophisticated of composers. For the lyrics, though, Porter turned to a poem he had bought in the 1930s from a genuine rider of the purple sage—for $200.

AMAZING GRACE

Words by John Newton; Music Traditional

TEMPO: Moderate   RHYTHM: None (Use single finger bass)   COLOR: Bagpipe, Oboe
Note: if you have the Bagpipe sound on your keyboard, hold down the F and C keys with the left hand and play the melody with the right hand.

Moderately

1. A - maz - ing___ grace, how sweet the sound that
2. 'Twas grace that___ taught my heart to fear. and
3. Through man - y___ dan - gers, toils and snares I

(1) saved a___ wretch like me.___ I once was lost but
(2) grace my___ fears re - lieved.___ How pre - cious did that
(3) have al - read - y come.___ 'Tis grace hath brought me

(1) now am found, was blind but___ now I see.___
(2) grace ap - pear the hour I___ first be - lieved.___
(3) safe thus far, and grace will___ lead me home.___

Additional Verses

How sweet the name of Jesus sounds
In a believer's ear;
It soothes his sorrows, heals his wounds,
And drives away his fear.

Must Jesus bear the cross alone
And all the world go free?
No, there's a cross for ev'ryone,
And there's a cross for me.

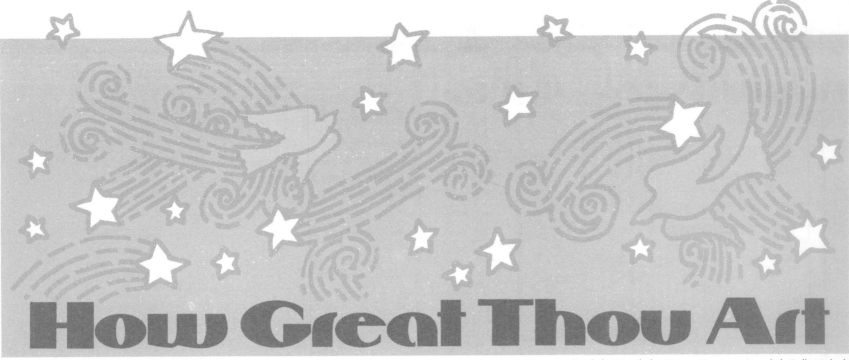

How Great Thou Art

English Words by Stuart K. Hine; Swedish Folk Melody

Slowly, with reverence TEMPO: Moderately slow and stately RHYTHM: None, play freely COLOR: Pipe Organ

1. O Lord, my God, when I in awe-some won — der _____ con-sid-er
2. When through the woods and for-est glades I wan — der _____ and hear the

(1) all the worlds Thy hands have made; _____ I see the stars, I hear the roll-ing
(2) birds sing sweet-ly in the trees; _____ When I look down from loft-y moun-tain

(1) thun — der, _____ Thy pow'r through-out the u-ni-verse dis-played. _____
(2) gran — deur _____ and hear the brook and feel the gen-tle breeze. _____

Additional Verses

And when I think that God, His Son not sparing,
Sent Him to die, I scarce can take it in;
That on the cross my burden gladly bearing,
He bled and died to take away my sin.
(Repeat Chorus)

When Christ shall come with shout of acclamation
And take me home, what joy shall fill my heart.
Then I shall bow in humble adoration
And there proclaim, my God, how great Thou art!
(Repeat Chorus)

Whispering Hope

Words and Music by Alice Hawthorne

TEMPO: Moderate   RHYTHM: Waltz (or none)   COLOR: Organ, Human Voice (Vox Humana)

✳ *The last 16 measures are played twice.*

ROCK OF AGES

Words by Augustus M. Toplady; Music by Thomas Hastings
TEMPO: Moderately slow   RHYTHM: Waltz (or none)   COLOR: Organ

Praise God from Whom All Blessings Flow

Words by Thomas Ken; Music by Louis Bourgeois

TEMPO: Slow and stately RHYTHM: None COLOR: Organ

Firmly

SHENANDOAH

Traditional

Freely

TEMPO: Slow   RHYTHM: None, play freely   COLOR: Harmonica, Oboe

1. Oh, Shen-an-doah,_____ I long to hear you,
2. Oh, Shen-an-doah,_____ I love your daugh-ter,
3. Oh, Shen-an-doah,_____ I'm goin' to leave you,

A-way, you roll-ing

(1) Oh, Shen-an-doah,_____ just to be near you,
riv-er. (2) Oh, Shen-an-doah,_____ a-cross the wa-ter,
(3) Oh, Shen-an-doah,_____ I won't de-ceive you,

A-way, we're bound a-

way, 'cross the wide Mis-sou-ri.

D. C.*

* Repeat from the beginning for additional words.

Copyright © 1991 Padmi Publishing Co.

175

Goodnight, Irene

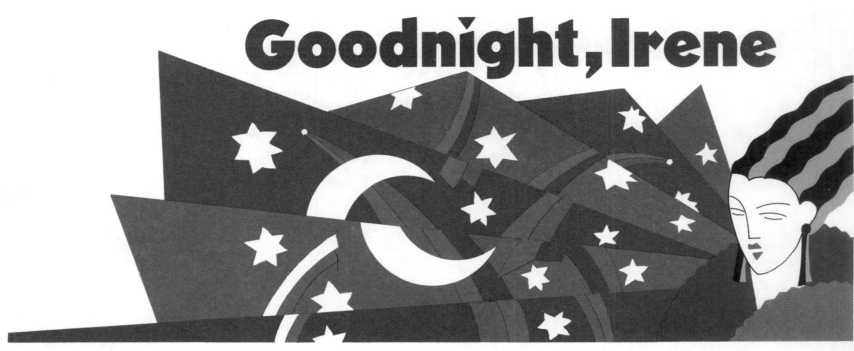

Words and Music by *Huddie Ledbetter* and *John Lomax*

TEMPO: Moderate   RHYTHM: Waltz   COLOR: Harmonica, Guitar

GREENSLEEVES

Traditional

TEMPO: Moderate   RHYTHM: Waltz   COLOR: Recorder, Pan Flute

Auto Bass Chord

Accord de basse automatique

Automatische Baß-und Akkordbegleitung

Single Finger

When this mode is selected, a chord with matching bass is obtained when you press a lower keyboard key with one finger.

* A major chord is obtained by pressing the key corresponding to the root.
* A minor chord is obtained by pressing the key corresponding to the root together with any black key to the left of it.
* A seventh chord is obtained by pressing the key corresponding to the root together with any white key to the left of it.
* A minor seventh chord is obtained by pressing three keys simultaneously -- the root key, plus any black and white key.

Doigt unique

Lorsque ce mode est choisi, un accord avec basse correspondante est obtenu quand on appuie sur une touche du clavier inférieur avec un doigt.

* *Un accord majeur est obtenu en appuyant sur la touche correspondant à la basse fondamentale.*
* *Un accord mineur est obtenu en appuyant sur la touche correspondante à la basse fondamentale en même temps qu'une touche noire à sa gauche.*
* *Un septième est obtenu en appuyant sur la touche correspondant à la basse fondamentale en même temps qu'une touche blanche à sa gauche.*
* *Un septième mineur est obtenu en appuyant trois touches simultanément ; la touche de basse fondamentale, plus une noire ou une blanche.*

Single Finger

Haben Sie diese Funktion gewählt, erhalten Sie einen Akkord mit dazupassendem Baß, wenn Sie eine Taste des unteren Manuals mit einem Finger anschlagen.

* Einen Dur-Akkord erhalten Sie, wenn Sie nur die Taste anschlagen, die dem Grundton entspricht.
* Einen Moll-Akkord erhalten Sie, indem Sie die Taste, die dem Grundton entspricht, anschlagen und dabei gleichzeitig eine beliebige schwarze Taste links davon.
* Einen Septakkord erhalten Sie, indem Sie die Taste, die dem Grundton entspricht, anschlagen und dabei gleichzeitig eine beliebige weiße Taste links davon.
* Einen Moll-Septakkord erhalten Sie, indem Sie drei Tasten gleichzeitig anschlagen, nämlich die für den Grundton sowie je eine beliebige schwarze und weiße Taste.

Fingered Chord

In this mode, a matching bass line and chord backing can be obtained by playing chords on the lower keyboard. The following chords can be obtained in the Fingered Chord mode: C, Cm, C_7, Cm_7, $C major_7$, Cdim, Caug, $Caug_7$, $Csus_4$, C_7sus_4, C_6, $Cm_7{}^{-5}$, C^{-5}, $C_7{}^{-5}$, Cm_6. Naturally, these basic chords can be played in the A-G range.

Accord doigté

Dans ce mode, on peut obtenir une ligne de basse et un appui d'accord en jouant les accords sur le clavier inférieur.
Les accords suivants peuvent être obtenus en mode Accord á plusieurs doigts C, Cm, C_7, Cm_7, $C majeur_7$, Cdim, Caug, $Caug_7$, $Csus_4$, C_7sus_4, C_6 $Cm_7{}^{-5}$, C^{-5}, $C_7{}^{-5}$, Cm_6. Bien entendu, ces accords fondamentaux peuvent être joués dans la gamme A-G.

Fingered Chord

Wenn Sie auf dem unteren Manual Akkorde anschlagen, erhalten Sie eine passende Baß-und Akkordbegleitung.
Die folgenden Akkorde können Sie mit der Fingered Chord-Funktion erhalten: C, Cm, C_7, Cm_7, $Cmajor_7$, Cdim, Caug, $Caug_7$, $Csus_4$, C_7sus_4, C_6, $Cm_7{}^{-5}$, C^{-5}, $C_7{}^{-5}$, Cm_6. Natürlich können diese Akkorde im Bereich von A bis G gespielt werden.

[Examples of Fingered Chords]

MC-400

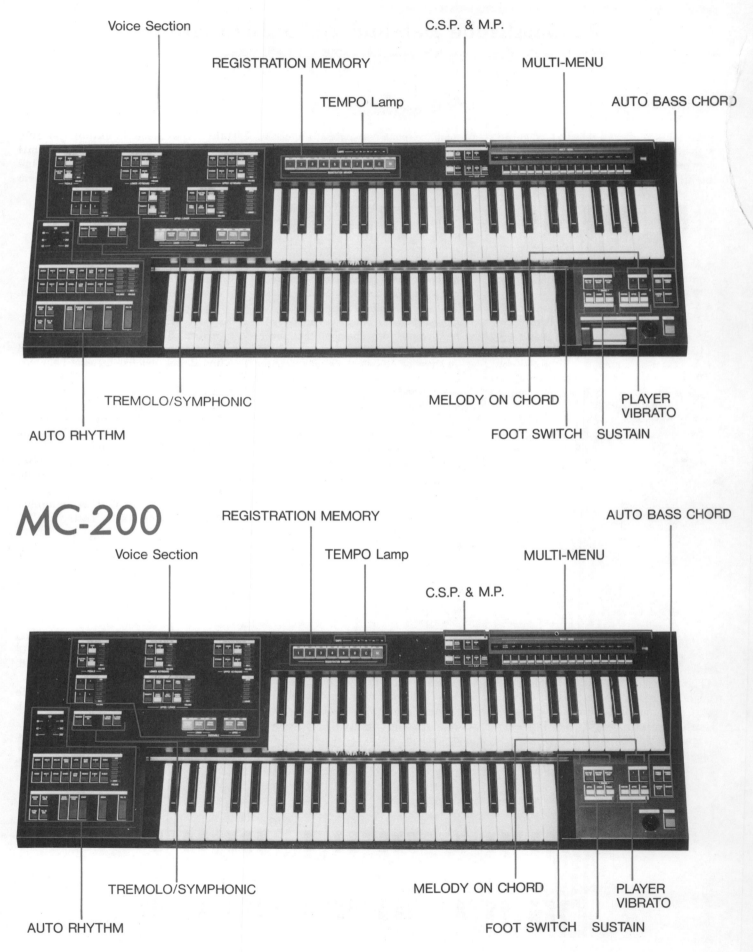

Voice Section

REGISTRATION MEMORY

TEMPO Lamp

C.S.P. & M.P.

MULTI-MENU

AUTO BASS CHORD

TREMOLO/SYMPHONIC

AUTO RHYTHM

MELODY ON CHORD

FOOT SWITCH   SUSTAIN

PLAYER VIBRATO

MC-200

REGISTRATION MEMORY

Voice Section

TEMPO Lamp

AUTO BASS CHORD

MULTI-MENU

C.S.P. & M.P.

TREMOLO/SYMPHONIC

AUTO RHYTHM

MELODY ON CHORD

FOOT SWITCH   SUSTAIN

PLAYER VIBRATO

5

I CAN'T STOP LOVING YOU

Words and Music by Don Gibson

TEMPO: Moderate   RHYTHM: Country   COLOR: Strings, Rock Organ

* This song begins on the 2nd beat of the measure.

Tennessee Waltz

Words and Music by Redd Stewart and Pee Wee King

TEMPO: Moderately slow   RHYTHM: Waltz   COLOR: Strings, Electric Guitar

Moderately slow waltz

Don't Fence Me In

Words and Music by Cole Porter

TEMPO: Moderately slow   RHYTHM: Country or Swing   COLOR: Banjo, Guitar

Loping along

Don't Fence Me In

188
GOD BLESS AMERICA

You know, "The Star-Spangled Banner" didn't officially become the national anthem of the United States until 1931. And if there's ever a referendum to replace it, one of the chief contenders will surely be Irving Berlin's hymn to his adopted country. The Russian-born composer never profited from this enduring classic. He donated all the royalties to the Boy Scouts and Girl Scouts of America.

190
AMERICA THE BEAUTIFUL

Katherine Lee Bates's "America the Beautiful" was a runner-up for U.S. national anthem back in 1931. Miss Bates was a professor of English who had been to Europe several times but hadn't seen much of her own country. When she made her first trip west, in 1893, she was awed by the view from the top of Pikes Peak in Colorado. She promptly wrote this stirring hymn of praise, which she elected to set to a stately tune by Samuel A. Ward.

191
THIS LAND IS YOUR LAND

In a sense, nobody ever really wrote this melody. Wandering minstrel Woody Guthrie adapted the music from two songs by the Carter Family, who in turn had borrowed the tune from an even older folk song. "This Land Is Your Land" was introduced by The Weavers in 1956 and helped to fire the folk music revival that soon followed.

192
DIXIE

"Dixie" has been a rallying cry for the South from Civil War days to the present, but the song was written by a Yankee, Ohio-born minstrel man Dan Emmett. In 1859, Emmett was performing with a troupe in New York City. As he sat in his boardinghouse one cold, rainy Sunday trying to write a closing song for the show, the dismal weather made him wish he were "in the land of cotton." The rest is part of history.

194
BATTLE HYMN OF THE REPUBLIC

The Northern equivalent of "Dixie" during the Civil War was the work of Julia Ward Howe, a poet, abolitionist and suffragette. She wrote "Battle Hymn of the Republic"—to the same tune as "John Brown's Body"—after touring an army camp near Washington, D.C., in 1861. Her poem was published the following year in the *Atlantic Monthly*, and has been a source of inspiration ever since.

196
ANNIVERSARY SONG

Written in 1880 by Romanian composer Ion Ivanovici, "Danube Waves" has long been a favorite at Jewish weddings. In 1947, Al Jolson and Saul Chaplin tried to capture that atmosphere for the film *The Jolson Story* and turned "Danube Waves" into "Anniversary Song." Larry Parks played the "world's greatest entertainer" on-screen, but Jolson did his own singing on the soundtrack. His recording of "Anniversary Song" became a best-seller.

198
LET ME CALL YOU SWEETHEART

Leo Friedman and Beth Slater Whitson made a mistake with their first song: in 1909 they sold "Meet Me Tonight in Dreamland" outright to the publisher. They got a few dollars; the publisher reaped a fortune when the tune sold more than 2 million copies of sheet music. The composers struck a better bargain the following year for "Let Me Call You Sweetheart": this time they got royalties on the 5 million copies sold.

200
RUDOLPH THE RED-NOSED REINDEER

Robert L. May, a copywriter for Montgomery Ward, wrote a little story about a reindeer with a bright red nose in 1939. Ten years later, songwriter Johnny Marks took the tale of Rudolph and created a Christmas classic. Singing cowboy Gene Autry's 1949 recording sold more than 2 million copies.

202
WINTER WONDERLAND

Richard Smith and Felix Bernard wrote this cozy ballad about the wonders of wintertime in 1934, but it wasn't until 1950 that the song became popular, thanks to a recording by The Andrews Sisters. Since then, it's been a perennial favorite.

204
AULD LANG SYNE

Scottish poet Robert Burns created this hymn to "old long ago" in the late 18th century. For 150 years, it was simply a song of the parting of friends. Then, on New Year's Eve in 1929, Guy Lombardo decided to play it at midnight. The song became so associated with New Year's Eve and with Lombardo that the bandleader used to joke: "When I go, New Year's Eve goes with me." It hasn't been the same without him.

205
HAPPY DAYS ARE HERE AGAIN

"Happy Days Are Here Again" is one of the first Depression-era songs, although it was written early in 1929, before the stock market crash in October. Its use was ironic, but it helped to lift spirits in those grim years and became Franklin D. Roosevelt's campaign song in 1932. Barbra Streisand took it up and made it a hit again in 1963.

208
HAPPY BIRTHDAY TO YOU

No, people haven't been singing "Happy Birthday to You" for hundreds of years. Sisters Patty and Mildred Hill, kindergarten teachers in Louisville, Kentucky, wrote it in 1893. Because it wasn't copyrighted until 1935, however, the song still earns royalties—up to $1 million a year. Not surprisingly, the *Guinness Book of World Records* lists it as one of the three most popular songs in the English language (along with "Auld Lang Syne" and "For He's a Jolly Good Fellow").

GOD BLESS AMERICA

Words and Music by Irving Berlin

TEMPO: Moderately slow   RHYTHM: March   COLOR: Brass Ensemble, Strings, Organ

America the Beautiful

Words by Katherine Lee Bates; Music by Samuel Augustus Ward

TEMPO: Moderate   RHYTHM: None (or very slow march)   COLOR: Organ

THIS LAND IS YOUR LAND

Words and Music by Woody Guthrie

With spirit   TEMPO: Moderate/Very fast   RHYTHM: March/Country   COLOR: Guitar, Banjo
(Change color on each successive chorus)

This song begins on the 2nd beat of the measure.

Additional Verses

I've roamed and rambled, and I followed my footsteps
To the sparkling sands of her diamond deserts.
And all around me a voice was sounding,
This land was made for you and me.

When the sun comes shining and I was strolling,
And the wheat fields waving and the dust clouds rolling;
As the fog was lifting, a voice was chanting,
This land was made for you and me.

DIXIE

Words and Music by Daniel Decatur Emmett

Spirited March

TEMPO: Moderately slow   RHYTHM: March   COLOR: Brass Ensemble, Flute

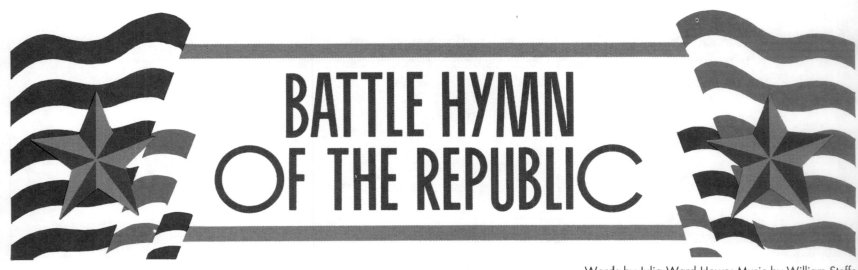

BATTLE HYMN OF THE REPUBLIC

Words by Julia Ward Howe; Music by William Steffe

Moderately slow march   TEMPO: Moderately slow   RHYTHM: March or without rhythm   COLOR: Organ, Brass Choir, Trumpet
(repeat chord on each beat)

1. Mine eyes have seen the glo-ry of the com-ing of the Lord; He is
2. I have seen Him in the watch fires of a hun-dred cir-cling camps, they have

(1) tram-pling out the vin-tage where the grapes of wrath are stored; He hath
(2) build-ed Him an al-tar in the eve-ning dews and damps, I can

(1) loosed the fate-ful light-ning of His ter-ri-ble swift sword; His
(2) read His right-eous sen-tence by the dim and flar-ing lamps; His

Additional Verses

He has sounded forth the trumpet that shall never sound retreat;
He is sifting out the hearts of men before His judgment seat;
O be swift, my soul, to answer Him! Be jubilant, my feet!
Our God is marching on.
(Chorus)

In the beauty of the lilies, Christ was born across the sea,
With a glory in His bosom that transfigures you and me.
As He died to make men holy, let us die to make men free,
While God is marching on.
(Chorus)

ANNIVERSARY SONG

Words by Al Jolson; Music by Saul Chaplin

TEMPO: Moderate   RHYTHM: Waltz   COLOR: Strings, Cello

1. Oh, how we danced on the night we were wed; We vowed our true love though a word was not said. The world was in bloom, there were stars in the skies, ex-

(2) night seemed to fade into blos - som - ing dawn, the sun shone a - new but the dance lin - gered on. Could we but re - live that sweet mo - ment sub - lime, we'd

*Repeat from the beginning and play through to the word "Fine." Use the second set of words.

LET ME CALL YOU SWEETHEART

Words by Beth Slater Whitson; Music by Leo Friedman

TEMPO: Moderate RHYTHM: Waltz COLOR: Strings, Organ

RUDOLPH THE RED-NOSED REINDEER

Words and Music by Johnny Marks

Moderately TEMPO: Moderate to Fast RHYTHM: Country or Swing COLOR: Toy or Electric Piano, Vibraphone

Ru-dolph the Red-Nosed Rein-deer had a ver-y shin-y nose, and if you ev-er saw it, you could e-ven say it glows. All of the oth-er rein-deer used to laugh and call him names; They nev-er let poor Ru-dolph join in an-y rein-deer games. Then one fog-gy

WINTER WONDERLAND

Words by Richard Smith; Music by Felix Bernard

Moderately, with a lilt

TEMPO: Moderate RHYTHM: Big Band, Swing COLOR: Strings, Accordion, Guitar

Sleigh bells ring; Are you list-'nin'? In the lane, snow is glis-t'nin', a beau-ti-ful sight,___ we're hap-py to-night ___ walk-in' in a win-ter won-der-land. Gone a-way is the blue-bird, here to stay is a new bird; He sings a love song___ as we go a-long,___ walk-in' in a win-ter won-der-land.

Auld Lang Syne

Words by Robert Burns; Music Traditional

TEMPO: Moderately   RHYTHM: None, or March   COLOR: Brass Choir, Organ or Bagpipe

Lyrics:

Should auld ac-quaint-ance be for-got and nev-er brought to mind? Should auld ac-quaint-ance be for-got and days of auld lang syne. For auld____ lang____ syne, my dear, for auld____ lang____ syne; We'll take a cup of kind-ness yet for auld____ lang____ syne.

Happy Days Are Here Again

Words by Jack Yellen; Music by Milton Ager

With a lift

TEMPO: Fast   RHYTHM: March/Polka   COLOR: Trumpet, Brass Ensemble

Hap - py days _____ are here a - gain! _____ The

skies a - bove _____ are clear a - gain. _____ Let us

sing a song _____ of cheer a - gain. _____ Hap - py

days are here a - gain! _____

Happy Days Are Here Again